The Novice Angler

poems by

J.M. Green

Finishing Line Press
Georgetown, Kentucky

The Novice Angler

Copyright © 2017 by J.M. Green
ISBN 978-1-63534-276-5 First Edition
All rights reserved under International and Pan-American Copyright Conventions.
No part of this book may be reproduced in any manner whatsoever without written permission from the publisher, except in the case of brief quotations embodied in critical articles and reviews.

ACKNOWLEDGMENTS

Thanks to the editors of the following publications where these poems first appeared, sometimes in slightly different forms:

Festival Writer: "Father Daughter Secret with Audrey"
Forklift, Ohio: "Unconditional Patience"
Ginger Piglet: "Easter at Nine," "The Novice Angler"
The League of Laboring Poets: "Six Rules for Strip Clubs"
Milk Money: "To explain my crusade"
MO: Writings from the River: "1976," "For My Student"
New Mirage Journal: "Bedroom Door," "Smallwood's Barbershop"
The New Verse News: "777 Miles from Sandy Hook Elementary School: December 14, 2012"
The Oklahoma Review: "From the Desk of a CIA Imagery Analyst"
Parks & Points: "Sherwood Park Community Club" first published as "Sherwood Park: Lima, Ohio"
Perspectives: "Bedroom Door" (reprinted)
Pudding Magazine: "night skies"
Puff Puff Prose, Poetry and a Play: "Pipes"
The Whistling Fire: "An Older Man & a Younger Man Discuss the Art of Poetry through the University Hedge" first published as "An Older Man & a Younger Man Discuss the Art of Poetry through the Zoo Hedge," "Witches"

Publisher: Leah Maines
Editor: Christen Kincaid
Cover Art and Design: Lizzy Achten
Author Photo: Paula Norton

Printed in the USA on acid-free paper.
Order online: www.finishinglinepress.com
        also available on amazon.com

Author inquiries and mail orders:
Finishing Line Press
P. O. Box 1626
Georgetown, Kentucky 40324
U. S. A.

Table of Contents

1976 1
Morning Memory 3
Easter at Nine 4
Smallwood's Barbershop 5
The Novice Angler 6
Pipes 7
An Older Man & a Younger Man Discuss the Art
    of Poetry through the University Hedge 8
Looking Down From My Apartment Window ... 11
Witches 12
Six Rules for Strip Clubs 14
From the Desk of a CIA Imagery Analyst 15
Bedroom Door 18
Her Stepfather's Time 19
For My Student 20
Sherwood Park Community Club 21
To explain my crusade 23
Grandma's Dirty Fingertips 24
777 Miles from Sandy Hook Elementary School ... 26
night skies 27
Unconditional Patience 28
With You 29
Father Daughter Secret with Audrey 30
Notes 31

For Nicki and Audrey, my two loves

1976

1

I sat with Gramps on the davenport.
We watched Ali claw Ken Norton for 15 rounds
On a 19-inch Philco & Gramps
Would rub my head & squeeze my toes.
Look how fast he is—that's why he's the champ.

2

In the garage I lined up the screwdrivers
According to length. I practiced
Pounding nails into wood scraps.
I built forts from folding chairs
& army blankets.
When I hid in the dryer,
Granny struck me on the bottom.
Don't you hide! Nothing good
Ever comes from sneaking around.
Later, after I'd snuck down the crawl space,
She pried my fingers from a chipmunk trap.

3

In the evening I would sit on the back porch
& watch Daddy, Gramps, & the men.
They drank beer & blew smoke. Sweat
Maneuvered through their whiskers.
Their necks & fingers were branded
Gray with foundry stains.
They called the neighbors
Around the corner beaners
& coons. I told them funny stories
About the boy across the street
I called Waltermelon & Walterbuffalo.

4
Gramps & I snuck off down the hill.
We walked through a corner of the woods
Like soldiers. Gramps whispered in a deep voice,
There's a bear, no, THERE'S a bear.
We marched across the iron bridge to conquer
The malt shop. We halted
Above the Wabash & Gramps pulled
An ivory handle from his pocket. He placed
His thumb on a little red button & slid
It forward while a blade became longer
& longer. I watched.
You put this right up to a nigger's belly—
& then slowly let the blade out.

Morning Memory

I feared the moment after we left the doctor's
office, after you dropped me off at the school's front
entrance, and before I opened the door to Mrs.
Hamblen's kindergarten class. I wanted to vomit.

Little monster heads turned; rays beamed from their eyes
creating a force field that suspended me mid air
until I hovered over my desk. When the heads snapped
back to their leader, I dropped to my seat, wounded.

We'd had such a good talk that morning. Why couldn't
we have stopped for ice cream and a matinee?
I would have paid because I knew you'd slip me money
later, and I would have held your hand like a date.

Do you remember how you spent the rest of that day?
I feared falling behind and remember nothing else.

Easter at Nine

I think, *you are a shit face*, even though
I'm sitting in God's house. And I am sure
God thinks you are a shit face too. He knows
that what you stole is melting in your
pocket—pants Mom *just* bought. Now, chocolate
smears all over that smile, even across
your cheek. And in your ear. That's why I hate
your shitty face. You say I'm not the boss
of you. But you just wait. Tonight I'll tell
God other stuff and he'll be more pissed
and might decide to send you right to hell.
I'll write to Santa—forget about his list!
I bet next year you won't think it's so funny
when I chew the head off *your* Easter bunny.

Smallwood's Barbershop

Balding men with stogies
And Saturday morning papers
Draped across their laps
Interrogate the teacher called Coach,
Who's drowning in foam and inexperience.

A little boy shops for a comic book.
He puffs on a long pretzel stick
Before pointing into a collage of frames
Scattered on the wall. His father answers:
*That's Larry; he's from around here,
Took the Trojans to Rose Bowls.
That's Neil; he's from around here,
Walked on the moon.*

Saddle soap crust and black speckles
Eat the creases of Hack's hands.
He spits on and buffs pointed wingtips
And faded loafers, while watching old war
Movies on a portable TV and compares
His rite of passage.

The little boy grabs a booster seat.
The barber pats on warm lather and shaves
With the backside of a straight razor
Before snipping the bangs. The barber
Hands a framed mirror to the little boy,
Who stares at his reflection—
Paying no attention to the haircut.

The Novice Angler

    1
Fascinated by the glow colors, he
sat American Indian style,
sifting through spoons and spinners, in an aisle
at the local tackle shop. Later, he
packed worms smashed in Styrofoam cups, rods, reels,
and beer onto a pontoon. He smiled—
a boy among uncles. Soon, they piled
northern pike into a well. The appeal
of men hooked the boy. He observed, listened:
Hey boy, God gave you the power to prey…
These strong men who quickly ripped hooks from mouths,
posed for pictures like couples, and christened
the fish wonderful friends, brothers. Then blades
sliced neatly through their backs while they still breathed.

    2
… and a man *uses his God given talent,*
so the boy spent the morning sticking bacon
treats on hooks and tying them to leaders.
Later, he took saltwater spinning rods
to a county rescue and trolled for pugs.
The boy caught two fawn bitches, but they were
too small—he threw them back. He was frustrated.
In the middle of the afternoon heat,
shih tzus did most of the bumping and nibbling.
The solitary boy stayed stubborn.
There was nothing like reeling in that thirty
pound black pug by his flap. He told classmates:
Might as well have been a damn rottweiler.
And they could see for themselves; a head mounted
alongside his uncle's little league plaque.

Pipes

Lawyers with heavily gelled pepper hair,
Wearing Easter-egg-colored ties
They adjusted in stained glass windows.
Local politicians with crippling handshakes
And Sunday morning compliments,
Slipping sticks of wintergreen
Stamped with campaign slogans
Into young palms.
And their women,
Sitting straight, and nodding
To acknowledge each other.

Finally—the organist began pounding keys.
From fog horn to the pitch of a coach's whistle,
There was a perpetual symphony of pipes.
Pipes able to encase a pinky finger,
Pipes able to encase a daddy figure.

And those old men shuffling down the aisle;
Hunching over with spectacles tipping off their noses,
Holding hymnals like scrolls.
Hymnals not like the congregation's,
But large, brass tipped, and leather bound.
Like their song, better than the parishioners',
Throats and bellies large, brass tipped, and leather bound.
Deep bellowing pipes of old men shouting:
Glory, glory, glory!
So much life in this church, yet only the pipes were of God.

An Older Man & a Younger Man Discuss the Art of Poetry through the University Hedge

> *Poetry is a pheasant disappearing in the brush.*
> —Wallace Stevens

1

When the old man was still a boy,
He stored his diploma in a drawer
Where it was safe and out of sight.

He worked job one to pay the bills;
Then two for the quatrefoil,
And three to start a better life.

But he worked best on a porch swing,
Or visiting kin he'd forgotten
And cities he had never been.

Along the way to this and that,
The man fell in love with pheasants
That flew over farm fields and ponds.

He studied them at the library
And then at the preserve. Finally,
He raised two—and they multiplied.

2

His ornate birds were asked to fly
Away; to be
Enjoyed
Over farm fields.

But one
Got away, hobbling through
The hedge
Separating the zoo

From the world. The man raced
To the hedge
And spread the branches
Best he could. Through the brush
He saw
A boy with naïve strides.

"Oh pardon me young man,
But my pheasant
Has escaped. How lucky
To find you here
On Sunday. You could
Be anywhere."

No sir. White smoke signals
Habemus Papam.
It's time—
News of the new
Game bird keeper.

    3
"Ah! A fellow Galliformes nerd.
Would you please help me find my bird?"

Well—that, kind sir, I cannot do;
It's now property of the zoo.

"Pheasants must fly across the plains—
Not subjected to wimps with chains."

That bird would die within a year
From Midwest hunters bored of deer.

"When birds escape a shot or two,
They're poked to death inside a zoo?"

        4
Pops, soon I'll explain to you your pheasant.
I know the experts through that portal.
This rescue will name me Immortal.

"What grand adventures you've had in your hedge.
What luck! You gain wisdom without exiting
The zoo. You understand without raising
The birds. You're content without following
Their flight in Sioux Falls or China; learning
In rooms where ideas bounce like buckshot.
Who among us will have the better thought?"

The boy could not answer—he was chasing
The pheasant in circles; the bird, darting
This way and that. The older man, scraping
His arms in the hedge, pushed back from the brush
And let the boy and pheasant disappear.
Thinking of birds, he walked toward anywhere.

Looking Down From My Apartment Window

I wiped breath from the glass to understand
why you walked away. At the florist shop,
you stooped to pick up a discarded pop
can, crushed by a foot or maybe a hand.
I never expected to see that. And
I never expected to see you stop
to pinch a cheek and pat the fluff on top.
What words did you recycle to command
such an innocent smile? And where was
my innocent smile? But when you rushed
down the sidewalk, anxious and unaware—
into a fenced area without pause
to notice *Hard Hats Required*, I blushed
for expecting that. My breath says I care.

Witches

When Missy hid my baseball cards I shoved
her face in mud, which proved—she said at twelve—
that mud packs cleanse the pores. "My face is soft
and you have zits." My date, amused, thought she
was cute when Missy rolled the window down
and yelled, "just kiss her, kiss her, use your tongue!"

My mother used her fingers, spit, and tongue
to give me cat baths on my face. She shoved
me back in line before they called me down
for my diploma. "Don't forget that twelve
is still your curfew, Mr. Big Shot," she
announced while serving ice cream, cake, and soft

drinks. Graduation night I chose Pam's soft
breasts, violating curfew for Pam's tongue
and fingers; coming in her bed when she
squeezed. During fall semester I was shoved
aside for education. I learned twelve
male tutors taught Pam tricks when they went down

on her. But soon I met perfection: down-
to-earth, great sense of humor, just a soft-
hearted girl. Then she got her rock and twelve
months later that heart petrified. My tongue
was cut, my balls were snipped, my pride was shoved
deep in the basement next to beer steins. She

would phone her mom twelve times a day. That she-
beast forced my wife and me to move our down-
town lives to Yentaville. There, the beast shoved
plump Mary Kay reps through our door with soft
scrub wands, potions, opinions. "Bite your tongue,"
I told myself. Instead I said "the twelve

disciples didn't baptize babes and twelve
disciples can't be wrong. My pumpkin—she'll
decide." The Mary Kay group cried. A tongue
lashing ensued. Pumpkin puked pea soup down
my throat. The hags screamed, "help us Lord; speak soft
words to thee!" To their cars they pushed and shoved.

Frog toes twelve start the spell. Add black bat down
and stir like hell. Then, she must whisper soft
in tongues—"unloved." And poof! AWAY he's shoved.

Six Rules for Strip Clubs

1
Never wear blue jeans!
If you want a *good* lap dance—
Prada, no khakis.

2
Only wear dark clothes!
Ultra-violet lights are strong—
tube socks never work.

3
You must wear a watch!
Show responsibility—
even if it's broke.

4
Wear designer shoes!
Girls can smell successful shoes—
watches leave no stench.

5
Wear enough cologne!
It shows proper hygiene and
masks your knock off shoes.

6
And no wedding ring!
This rule should be obvious—
but keep it close by.

From the Desk of a CIA Imagery Analyst

I choose to live like a mole, fashioning myself a freedom fighter
    against a future dominant
power. In an obscure building, on a dark vaulted floor, in a corner
    cubicle, under a single light, I fight the villain
Dear Leader, the Korean Lex Luther, with the super powers of satellite
    photos. I'm prudent
with national security, knowing my secrets are for safety.
    And I romanticize
that my eyes might change the world—if only some politician or
    media mogul writes Kim Jong-il
on his weekly agenda. Until then, my intelligence will be typed and
    stored into a database and will extrude,

I'm sure, much too late. Yet I will be blamed—as I am for my penis.
    Exuberance
has evaporated from my sex life, naturally, since my penis has gone
    soft. Because I don't dominate
in the bedroom, I no longer call it a dick or my piece. Those seem like
    strong words. My wife placed jonquils
in the bedroom. She read their scent was an aphrodisiac. Our last
    hope. But, those vile
weeds made me ill. I wish I were a tyrant. Not a Kim but a Caesar
    with a Roman size
erection—and wrapped in my bed sheets. My wife would marvel
    at how it protrudes

well beyond the folds of cotton. But, alas, I see no protrusion.
I've looked at magazines: partial nude, full nude, soft nude, hard
    triple X nude.
I feel nothing. I'm limp, like lettuce. Mr. Romaine
she calls me. I need a sex therapist. No, a dominatrix.
But I hate pain, mental and physical. Anyway, I'll sit and flap
    my legs in an uncivil
manner, hoping for a reaction, and try to spot unusual activity
    from Kim Jong-il.

        That fucking Kim Jong-il!
        His obelisks protrude
        from North Korean vil-
        lages where they exude
        his virile dominance.
        A Kim third world romance.

        More orgy than romance
        perhaps. A vast jungle
        of tank gun arrogance.
        It seems a little crude,
        all these shafts for one dude.
        Dictators make me ill.

I'll choose to scan a couple more photos before suffocating
    from servility.
Then, I'll cram into the Metro and scurry across a romantic
landscape of cherry blossoms. I'll blur the image of that vulgar
    monument, as I hope I'm excluded
from the vision of the blossom-eaters. Please don't notice my guilt.
Please don't notice the giant "I" sewn on my chest. See, I'm
    no pro—true
to justice and the American way. This "I" isn't for Imageryman.
    I'm dominated

by a curse, not super powers. If I'm cursed am I more villain than Kim Jong-il?
Excuse me, but I've been told I'm not a man if I'm dominated by the intelligence stored in my one-eyed willy.
Yet, without my protrusion, I am NoMan. I see nothing.

Bedroom Door

Forget I felt the slams.
One side of me saw her pain,
the other felt your fists,
pounding for another chance.
I prayed you'd both get it.
Did I delay forgiveness?
I wanted to get it right.

I felt her push me gingerly
one night, whispering good-bye.
I did my best, didn't I?
I would shut the world out,
then open again.

When I creaked
you silenced me with oil.
Didn't you know I was trying
to tell you something?
The sneaking in, the sneaking out.

The emptiness of space
before you carried her through:
something about that moment
when life changes.
I most enjoyed the times
you were both tucked in
and I was closed.

Her Stepfather's Time

He never answered: I only have a few minutes. Instead,
He gave up a relaxing lunch and mom's homemade bread

To bear the burden of a burger, fries,
And Coke and late arrival apologies.

He never asked: When will you stop that damn crying?
Instead, he requested his abused toolbox hiding

In the backyard fort, where it had been defending
Itself against rust since early Easter morning.

He never glanced at his wrist and mumbled: I'm in a rush, maybe this
Weekend. Instead, he held one hand tight on a wrench while his

Other hand cranked a ratchet. His minute and hour hands were shackled
To a button and fob buried deep in his suit vest pocket. He never snapped:

Not now! I have important things to attend to.
Instead, he asked: Honey, I realize you

Are busy, but do me a favor and call my clients
And, please, postpone my afternoon appointments.

He always patted her head and gave her a smile.
He knew repairing this problem might take them awhile.

He wasn't the man who bought the bike, but he took the time to fix it.

For My Student

My day begins after the final bell—
waiting for your visits. You always rest
your chin on my desk and ask me to tell
you about the world. And I try my best
to show you concern, while hiding my joy
when you lament about friends or a boy.
Yes! My role as problem solver—hero.
Perhaps my day ends when we say goodbye,
and the hand that cups your shoulder lets go.
At home I ask questions—but she won't reply.
I'd love *your* chin on my dinner table.
Before you'd stroll to bed, we'd be able
to hug. Then you would say, "I love you too."
I have a daughter. But I'd prefer you.

Sherwood Park Community Club

Looking back, I concede these were not
Major luxuries. A large L-shaped pool,
Two diving boards and a slide—
But swim meets in the evenings,
And days when junior high
Crushes brushed against each
Other, during water games.

Near the baby pool, elementary
School teachers congregated
To complain about children,
While rocking their own.
Retired auto plant workers sat
In a circle of lawn chairs
Drinking beer until a teenaged
Lifeguard received a call
At the desk. A chirpy voice then
Would flutter through the intercom:
"Mr. McClure, your wife wants
You home for dinner" or "Mr.
Graham, she says she's having
A hard time getting the
Wallpaper to put itself up."

It had a clubhouse:
Fourth of July dances,
Neighborhood meetings
Where they debated and decided
Official club colors.
Only three tennis courts
But hours of lessons, round robins.
The reservation board hung
On the chain link fence
Got stored in a shed years before
The nets were rolled up.

If I could just mount a horse,
Ride to those areas outside town,
Once covered with corn and
Soybean fields, rob the land
Of those holes—not all eighteen,
But a few of the smaller pars—
And several of the hot tubs
Planted in decks and scattered
Around cul-de-sacs, then throw
Them into my bag, toss them
Inside the crumbling white brick
wall, I damn sure would.

To explain my crusade

it's mowing fields
of dripping blades

and I must pause
with every step
I take and tilt
the mower back
before it stalls

but soon it stalls
because I'm not quick

I want to pull
the start cord once
and try to keep
a steady pace
complete the job

Grandma's Dirty Fingertips

As a little girl, Grandma's
Wee fingertips were pricked with splinters
From whittled brooms she used to sweep up floors
And deadbeats. Other children's fingertips
Were smudged with pencil lead, but a film of dust
Had coated Grandma's. Soon the desert dust
Raced through her nicotine stained fingertips
When Grandma, Grandpa, and their children drove west,
Searching for something better. Something better
For Grandma was the operator switchboard jacks
That pressed into her fingertips at night.
Early mornings she soothed them
By holding a thin wooden paintbrush.
Her palettes bloomed lush gardens, ocean waves,
Churches and bridges and places she planned to go.
These worlds she painted were full of life,
But never people. When she was older
Grandma's fragile fingertips pressed a Bible
Or loose topsoil that smelled of boxwoods.
Her cuticles were waxed with slivers from
Yardley English lavender—soaps
She kept in drawers and closets. We inhaled
Her fingertips when she would pat our cheeks:
Those fingers laced with turkey grease, korv,
And potions mixed from rice, cinnamon and cream.
Grandma's fingertips were stained pale green.
She put the squeeze on stacks of cash.
By the end, I found tiny threads under
Her fingernails from digging at the arms
Of her old easy chair. Detritus left
On Grandma's fingers, I scrubbed clean
With boxwood loofahs and lavender soaps.

But since then, my Grandma's fingerprints
Have reappeared. They're on the back
Of mother's hand—and on my brother's too.
I've yet to see the dirty prints on me
But I've been told they're there—as when I write.

777 Miles from Sandy Hook Elementary School
December 14, 2012

I.
Had lunch with Jim. It'd been like months. We shelved
work shit—talked girls, our little girls. A choice
unspoken. Something eyes and breaths just delved
into. His talk: importance of her voice
when boys round first base. Mine: importance of
her keeping track of mittens. We agreed
joyful and kind were virtues far above
"gifted." By God our ladies better bleed
real empathy and social justice! Jim
shared family stuff he never shared before.
The secret turned to silence, not a grim
silence, but strong silence with dad rapport.
We laughed down Ludlow Avenue, both bugged
by Christmas pop songs. We shook hands then hugged.

II.
I drove off, pressed for time. This day was my
day—carpool pick up. We drive because of
school cut backs. More recession bullshit I
adjust my day for. News brooded above
the dashboard like a gray haze. Blindly I
fell in the carpool line at Heritage
Elementary. Not the same school some guy,
no, some crazy fucking psychopath barged
into killing our kids. A saved school for
now—thank God. Parents sat in their cars, I
saw, staring through their hazes. My car doors
opened—Audrey and the neighbor girls—I
switched channels quick. They jumped right into song
with Mariah's Christmas wish. I stayed strong.

night skies

how the night sky's ceanothus
not the black crayon
I used in grade school art class
thirty some years ago.
Finally, I find peace
with midnight's blue
the tuxedo color my friend
Chris wore at our senior prom
because midnight blue was cheaper than black
because his parents found
"A Night in (insert that year's European city)"
not worth the money
and the guys around the table
gave Chris such a hard time
but he smiled anyway
danced all night on the gym floor
under the mirror ball
silver screen handsome.

Unconditional Patience

Thank you for the gifts my pretty angels.
Thank you for a wonderful Father's Day.
Thank you, Pumpkin, for the tie you purchased
With your allowance. You helped clean dishes
And gathered clippings from the flower beds.
I watched you store half your coins in a porcelain
Pig because you want to go to college.
And the other half, you saved for my tie.
I'm so proud of you. And thank you, Sweet Pea,
For the other tie. You reminded me
That I never wear this tie. You found it
Buried deep in my closet as you scrounged
For something else. You wrapped it with duct tape
And newspaper all by yourself. I like
It better now than when Grandma gave it
To me. I'm so proud of you. And thank you,
My Little Pistol, for the fish. No one
Has ever given me a fish. We live
Nowhere near water, and yet, on my lap
Is a dead fish. What magnificent stripes.
And the scales are so shiny. I'm going
To get that chain you gave me for Christmas,
The one you found in the neighbors' backyard
Hooked to their dog, and I'm going to wear
My fish on casual Friday. I'm proud
Of you too. I'm so proud of all of you.

With You

I thought there was nothing as beautiful as you; but
I was wrong, I discovered after snorkeling in Kealakekua Bay.
Your brown curly hair isn't as interesting as the redshoulder
Wrasse splashed with peachy pink, blue, and yellow watercolors.
Your eyes? Dull and pale after gliding over green sea turtles.
Even your smooth skin cannot compare to the sleek spotted
Eagle ray; I was lost in its labyrinth of onion rings.
A big bucket of onion rings I'll eat
While you sip Moscato d'Oro with this old mud puddle
On our porch after a day of snorkeling in Kealakekua Bay.

Father Daughter Secret with Audrey

We share a secret you and me. And you
decided not to tell your mom. And we
made pinky promises to take it to
the grave. And sometimes I wonder can she
pull this off. Then I see you act. You're like
your name sake, playing pious to the script.
I'm fooled as well, especially when you strike
from nowhere, speak with nonchalance, then flip
your hair and walk away. And thank you. Thank
you for the moments when you interrupt
my absentminded grown up thoughts. You spank
my backside gently, shed shyness, corrupt
my distance—you desire daddy's space.
Your wink: reminder of our secret's grace.

Notes

"Smallwood's Barbershop" is dedicated to the late Dick Smallwood.

"An Older Man & a Younger Man Discuss the Art of Poetry through the University Hedge" is written after "Peter Quince at the Clavier," by Wallace Stevens (1879-1955).

"Six Rules for Strip Clubs" is for EWR.

"For My Student" is written after "For My Daughter," by Weldon Kees (1914-1955).

"Grandma's Dirty Fingertips" is dedicated to the late Velma Carlson.

"Witches" is the concluding poem in a sestina series from the chapbook *Super Rich*.

"Unconditional Patience" is for Richard Covault.

"With You" is for Nicole Green.

"1976" won first prize from the Writer's Center at Chautauqua Poetry Contest, 2006.

As a group, "For My Student," "The Novice Angler," "Pipes," "Smallwood's Barbershop," and "With You" placed second from the English Department, University of Cincinnati's Jean Chimsky Poetry Prize, 2007.

J.M. Green wrote "In the Line of Duty" for *Cincinnati* magazine in 2010. He is a graduate of The Ohio State University, University of Cincinnati, and University of Kentucky. He has spent most of his professional life "career exploring," which has included trash collecting for Waste Management, serving as a Marine infantry officer and as a CIA analyst, and teaching high school English. He is now a librarian at Xavier University. For the past three years, he has served as a judge for the Ohioana Poetry Award from the Ohioana Library in Columbus. For more information visit jmgreenauthor.com.

www.ingramcontent.com/pod-product-compliance
Lightning Source LLC
LaVergne TN
LVHW041604070426
835507LV00011B/1304